Coaching Questions:

200 Breakthrough Questions for Career and Business Mastery

Gerald Confienza

Table of Contents

A Gift for You

Most of the material I write about is centered on developing our inner selves. Thus, as you might've guessed, my readers are usually introverts. Being an introvert myself, I'm aware of our shortcomings. This is why I have decided to gift you with some amazing material for your growth. By simply clicking the link below, you will have access to the *Introvert Survival Kit* and *Inward Thrive* Email Series for free.

Visit the following site or click here for full access: http://bit.ly/introvertsk This powerful bundle will help you make massive improvements in your social life. It contains 3 Ebooks and 2 articles:

- EBook 1: Making and Keeping Friends: Developing Friendships that Last a Lifetime in this Fast Paced World!
- EBook 2: How to Stop Worrying and Start Living Effectively In the 21st Century: An Updated Guide to Living Free of Worry in the Knowledge Era
- EBook 3: High Impact Communication: Tips on Getting Your Strongest Message Across in 1 Minute
- Article 1: How to Break the Cycle of Anxiety and Enjoy Social Situations
- Article 2: Be an Introvert and Have an Active Social Life

I'd recommend not missing out! Just go to: http://bit.ly/introvertsk

I also have a special invitation for those appreciate a good read. If you'd like to be part of the review process of many of our upcoming books (and receive free copies!), and click here: http://bit.ly/itadvancedreview I will send you details of what it entails through mail. Thanks!

Coaching Yourself with Self-Questioning: Introduction

Back in the days when I was still in the telecom industry, I met someone – an enthusiastic, dream-filled man in his early 30s. Let's call him Jack. We may not have had the luxury of time to hang out outside of work, but we regularly caught up whenever we had the chance- usually during lunch breaks. He was an admirable family man. He was the kind of husband who'd spend his days off lending his wife a hand; the kind of father who'd take initiative to play with his 3-year-old son, the kind of guy who'd always decline our colleagues' invitations to hang out during weekends. I had been working there a few months when he came, and his occasional queries about reports paved the way for our budding friendship. Everything was a smooth sailing for us and the rest of our team. That all changed when upper management decided to transfer him to another department.

In just a few months, I saw his drastic transition from a cheerful go-getter to someone who rarely smiled at the office. I heard the financial department was a stressful place to be in, but I didn't realize how serious it was until I saw him in that state. When I finally had the chance to speak with him, he vented out how mentally and physically draining his new tasks were, not to mention he had a few work-related issues with some colleagues. At times, despite not being able to get enough rest, he was even worried to call in sick because he just didn't want to be confronted by his very strict supervisor. I advised him to file a short vacation leave just to loosen up, you know, set priorities straight. The way I saw it, he had them all tangled up. It would a short leave to reward himself for everything he had to endure on a daily basis. He tapped me on the shoulders, smiled, and said: *"Man, I couldn't afford to take one."* All he wanted was to provide a permanent home for his family and finally stop spending on monthly rentals. So despite the hefty workload and stressful environment, he continued working and promised to stop only when he had enough savings to pay for that small condominium unit he'd been eyeing.

A couple more months have passed, and his health started to decline. Too much exhaustion caused him some physical discomfort, in addition to his unstable blood pressure. I did my best to talk him out of that unhealthy work routine, to no avail. He wanted to earn more but totally forgot to invest in good health which is an essential factor for anyone's success. As a friend, I wanted him to realize that our savings would be useless if, at the end of the day, we're just going to spend it on sustaining our medications, all because we took our health for granted.

But as much as I wanted to continue monitoring his situation, some personal stuff came up and I needed to pursue other things. I left the company, hoping to one day catch up with my previous workmates, especially Jack. My friend clearly had a good intention, but it didn't necessarily lead him to good results, which sometimes made me wonder, *"Where did Jack go wrong?"*

He focused on his goals to the point that he became oblivious to his own needs, both physiological and emotional. His judgment was clouded with the unbalanced desire to be successful. *He had clear goals but had lost sight of the larger picture.* Why? A great navigator must triumph over the daily problems that may affect a ship. However, no matter how arduous these become, a navigator must never lose sight of the destination. The destination for Jack may have been buying a condo, but what did that condo really represent? It represented a home, a place where he and his family could enjoy and feel the security of a having a place that's truly theirs. However, if the provider, in this case, Jack, falls ill, sacrifices his emotional and psychological well-being in the process, and becomes unable to keep providing for his family, then what? Then all of Jack's efforts become in vain. *All because Jack never took the time to stop, breathe and ask himself the right questions.*

I wrote this book as an invitation for my dear readers to do just that. As we progress in anything, it inevitably becomes routine. When we're in a routine, our minds become fixed and we tend to think there's only one way to reach a certain outcome. Think about it. I'm sure we could all agree that, had Jack taken the time to sit down and think about other ways of getting what he wanted, he could've come up with something. Jack could've easily asked for his old position back and have started a side business to make up for the income reduction. He could've started an online business as a side project. He could've negotiated fewer hours. He could've been honest to his superiors about his declining health and motivation. He could've looked for another job. The point is, the world is not black and white, nor is the acquisition of our life's objectives fixed in only one possible path.

It's because of this that I have designed this book to be an interactive, almost journal-like, series of questions to encourage self-discovery in one of the most important areas of our lives which is our occupation. Self-awareness is a powerful tool we need to acquire and it's something you can start incorporating into your life with just one question a day. Experts agree that coaching yourself through questions is a powerful tool to self-discovery. World-renowned coach Anthony Robbins always tells us in his seminars that the quality of our lives depends on the quality of the questions we ask ourselves. He's not wrong. And so, I encourage you to go through these questions (or study them so you can have others go through them), let go of any filters and respond with full honesty. Like a journal, answer one or two questions a day.

"Your choices decide your fate. Take the time to make the right ones."
- Unknown

Benefits of Self-Awareness

Aristotle once said, "knowing yourself is the beginning of all wisdom". This statement hits it right on the mark. Due to the educational system we grew up in, we were fed ideas about success that aren't necessarily true anymore. The idea of graduating college, getting a job, and keeping it for 40 years is rapidly becoming outdated. Opportunities for career or business growth are now more abundant than ever before in the history of humanity. Because of this, we must be aware of our needs, our talents, our desires both in the workplace and out if we want to embark on a path of growth, whichever that may be. Knowing what it is that you want will give you an edge over everyone else. You will give a sense of direction and purpose, while most will continue their living in reaction to whatever cards life deals them.

However, it doesn't stop there. Coaching yourself through self-questioning will help you, for instance, become a better decision maker. When practiced regularly, it will help you recognize the grey areas of your character and conduct let you know what you need to work on. When you have a better understanding of your desires, shortcomings, habits, and priorities, you will be empowered to initiate changes. The more aware you are of yourself, the better you'll understand your reasons behind your own decisions.

The Gift of Having a Purpose

There is a fine line between living and merely surviving. Having a definite set of goals that make you enthusiastically leap out of bed every morning; that, my friend, is living. When getting through the work week seems like a very difficult task, and you find solace on the promise of the weekend, then you are probably just trying to survive. Sit down. Think. Are you pleased with your life as it is? Is that really what you are going to do for the rest of your life? Successful people acquired success not because they had it all figured out. It's because they sat down and discovered their purpose. And once they identified it, they went in pursuit of it.

This is the gift of self-awareness- the ability to pursue something with abandonment because you know it's taking you where you really want to be, not because people around you dictate you to do so. Thus, self-awareness and life purpose go hand in hand.

Tips to Keep in Mind

I encourage you to complete this book and reflect on the things that matter most; to look inside yourself and be honest about the confusion you're going through without being embarrassed about it. Sometimes, in the process of self-discovery, we tend to judge ourselves in a punitive manner and are usually overly critical about our faults. This is not the correct mindset to approach the questions as they will only lead to a state of helplessness. Negativity is something we must avoid if we seek growth in any aspect of life.

Don't judge yourself too harshly. Instead, we invite you to take a more self-reflective approach and acknowledge the things that could have caused your shortcomings. Be nonjudgmental about rejections, accept the fact that everyone gets to experience failure, and prepare yourself to succeed in the next occasion. As Anthony Robbins would say, "See things as they are, but not worse than they are."

How to Use These Questions to Coach Others

When you think about leaders that have worked with you and impacted your life, what is it that you remember about them? Is it their performance during operations? Is it their perfect attendance? Or perhaps all the papers you were asked to submit? Not at all. What you remember is how they tried to connect with you – the genuineness and the ability to understand you on a deeper perspective as a person, not just an employee. That is how a leader makes an impact on his or her people's life and that is the idea that should be sub-communicated in the practice of coaching others.

Using the questioning method to coach other people requires two things: recognizing *what good leaders do* and learning *what the right questions* are. If you are able to fully understand these two, it will give you a clear framework for approaching those who need your advice.

What Good Leaders Do

What do good leaders do when coaching others? Though there's a lot taking place when a leader coaches someone, we can summarize them into three things:

1. First, a leader must be equipped with the ability to empathize with his people.
2. A good leader must lead their people into honest self-reflection.
3. A good leader must coach his people without destructive criticism or a personal agenda.

To put it simply, coaching is just having a sincere conversation with your people and asking them powerful questions to address, and hopefully resolve, their shortcomings. It doesn't have to be in form of a seminar or meeting, just an engaging one-on-one talk or any set-up that is most comfortable for the both of you. Just make sure that you keep those three points in mind when attempting to coach others with the questions you will encounter in this book.

Asking the Right Questions

To ask the right questions is to avoid putting the individual in an uncomfortable situation. Asking *why* can be crucial, as it can be judgmental or too confrontational, especially if not delivered carefully. Open-ended, on the other hand, can be more encouraging. If an employee makes a mistake, asking him "What was your intention with that?" sounds more empathetic than simply asking "Why did you do it?" The wrong questions may only stir up our negative emotions.

But aside from choosing the right questions and proper deliverance, the most important thing is to show that you are genuinely curious to hear their answers. Not because that's what you are supposed to do according to the rules, but because genuinely care for the other's wellbeing.

Tips to Keep in Mind

The act of asking instead of suggesting may be the foundation of this method, but its success does not entirely rely on the right questions. When approaching somebody for coaching, your main goal should be to evoke a sense of certainty and awareness in the other. Your willingness to listen to the answers and your ability to decipher the emotions encrypted in every word (as not everyone will be comfortable to open up immediately) and to adapt your approach accordingly will facilitate the coaching process.

EMPLOYEES: *On People and Professional Relationships*

"The road to success and the road to failure are almost exactly the same."

1.) How comfortable are you with your co-workers? Who do you usually hang out with during lunch breaks? Does being with these people (or person) contribute to your happiness in the workplace? And if so, in what way?

2.) List down 5 workmates whom you consider your closest friends at work. What do you do to please them (or to please a friend in general)? How important do you think interpersonal relationships are in the workplace?

"Success is not final; failure is not fatal: It is the courage to continue that counts."

3.) What other interests do you share with your co-workers that are not related to work? How did you discover these similarities? Given a chance, what activities would you like to do with your co-workers that may help you unwind and loosen up?

4.) Give at least 3 kinds of traits that you look for in an ideal teammate. How important are these traits to you? And how do you think these traits will affect your performance in general?

"Opportunities don't just happen; you create them."

5.) On a scale of 1 to 5, how comfortable are you in terms of opening up to your superior? Try to give at least 3 factors that make you feel either at ease or uneasy (depending on the rate you've given) around these people. Please elaborate on each.

6.) List down 5 behaviors that you think people might not like about you. Which one do you think could be the worst? How do you feel about these behaviors? Do you think it is something that you can actually work on?

"The most successful men in the end
are those whose success is the result of steady accretion."

7.) What forms of gesture or body language do you consider as signs that people do not like you? How do you feel about it? And how do you handle the thought that some people might not like you for what you are?

8.) List down or think of 3 misunderstanding incidents you've had with a co-worker in the past. Next, reflect on the biggest one. What did you do to resolve the issue? Were you happy or satisfied with the way you handled the situation?

"Nothing reinforces a professional relationship more than enjoying the success with someone."

9.) Think of any (small) misunderstanding or argument you once had with your superior. What had been the reason for this? How did you manage to explain yourself without escalating the tension? Were you satisfied with the way you handled the situation?

10.) Misunderstandings at the workplace are inevitable, but what exactly is your mindset towards this? How do you try to avoid miscommunication with your co-workers? And what is the importance of addressing work-related issues immediately?

EMPLOYEES: On Achievements and Failures

"I find that the harder I work, the more luck I seem to have."

11.) Recall at least 3 achievements you've reached in the past couple of years. Which among these do you consider the largest? How did you manage to achieve it? Were there any sacrifices that had to be done in order to obtain it?

12.) Give at least 3 "smaller" achievements you had this (or last) year. How did they help you come up with a fresher work perspective? How do small things actually contribute to a bigger success?

"There are two types of people who will tell you that you cannot make a difference in this world: those who are afraid to try and those who are afraid you will succeed."

13.) What do you do to celebrate achievements? And how do celebrations help you in terms of maintaining your enthusiasm towards your work?

14.) What piece of advice can you give someone who wanted to achieve something in his professional life, but is being discouraged by his failures in the past?

15.) How does an achievement, no matter how small or big it is, change someone's perspective towards work? How did your own professional achievement change yours?

16.) What particular task do you feel you actually failed at? What do you think could be the reason for this? And given a chance, how would you handle the same task to get a better result?

"I owe my success to having listened respectfully to the very best advice, and then going away and doing the exact opposite."

17.) Think about the 3 most recent work-related failures you had. What did you learn from these events, personally and professionally? How do you think these experiences could help you become a better person?

18.) It is innate for us to celebrate achievements, but how do you usually handle failures? Do you think failures can be looked at in a positive way? And if so, what do you do in order to absorb it without being discouraged?

"If you are not willing to risk the usual, you will have to settle for the ordinary."

19.) How would you encourage someone to not lose hope after failing at something? Do you think relaying your personal story of failure may actually help encourage an individual to try again and start anew? If so, what would be your approach on this?

20.) On a scale of 1 to 5, how comfortable are you in terms of discussing a task you failed at with your superior? How do you think this kind of discussion may help you do better next time?

EMPLOYEES: On Short and Long-Term Goals

"If you really look closely, most overnight successes took a long time."

21.) List down at least 5 short-term, professional goals you wish to achieve this year. In how long (weeks or months) do you wish to achieve each goal? What course of action do you plan in order to accomplish them?

22.) List down at least 3 long-term, professional goals you wish to achieve in the coming years. In how many years do you wish to achieve each goal? What course of action do you plan in order to accomplish them?

"The successful warrior is the average man, with laser-like focus."

23.) What do you think is the importance of setting smaller goals before going for the bigger ones? When can you consider a goal as short-term? How about as long-term?

24.) How do you see yourself in about 5 years? What significant changes do you wish to acquire in your life, both personal and professional, by this time? Do you still see yourself in the same line of work, or perhaps get your feet wet on a different field?

"Character cannot be developed in ease and quiet. Only through experience of trial and suffering can the soul be strengthened, ambition inspired, and success achieved."

25.) How do goals affect our mindset towards work? Do you think setting a particular goal make us mentally stronger? If so, in what way?

"Fall seven times; stand up eight."

26.) What do you usually do to unwind? Do you think that social activities can actually affect an individual's professional performance? In what way do you think it contributes to your creativity at work?

27.) When you are neither working nor socializing, how do you usually relax at home? What does personal space mean to you? And how do you think having your personal space may contribute to your ability to work better?

"Our greatest weakness lies in giving up. The most certain way to success is always to try just one more time."

28.) Think of at least 5 nonwork-related topics you enjoy talking about with your family or friends. How do these things make you happy? How healthy do you think it is to wander your mind off the work-related stories and stuff?

29.) Most jobs can be sedentary. What do you do (or at least intend to do) in order to maintain your physical health during your days off? How do you think a good physical condition may help us accomplish a lot more at work?

"Travel and change of place impart new vigor to the mind."

30.) When you think of a vacation leave, what activities come to your mind? How often do you wish you could unwind?

EMPLOYEES: On Self-Improvement

"A successful man is one who can lay a firm foundation with the bricks that others throw at him."

31.) On a scale of 1 to 5, how happy are you right now in terms of career? Is there anything in particular that you wish to change about your work routine? How will this affect your performance and happiness in the workplace?

32.) List down 5 good skills (work-related) that are proven to help you with your daily work routine. Which among these do you consider the best? What new skills would you like to develop that may satisfy you professionally?

"The only place where success comes before work is in the dictionary."

33.) Think of the recent challenges you have encountered at work. How do you think challenges can be a good way to push someone to become more strong-willed? How do you usually handle challenges in your personal and professional life?

34.) What is the essence of having a particular role model to observe? Who do you look up to in terms of professional success? When do you think an individual should carry out changes to further improve himself?

"Be so busy improving yourself that you have no time to criticize others."

35.) Think of the challenges you've had recently. When was the last time you felt the need to change and improve yourself? What was the reason behind this? Whose advice do you seek in times like this?

"Find somebody to be successful for. Raise their hopes. Think of their needs."

36.) What kind of work culture would you like to create, if given a chance? How do you think the culture in the workplace affects people's perspective towards work in general? What are the elements of a good working environment?

37.) What do you think could be the reasons for someone to lose his motivation to work? And if you are in the position to help, how would you bring out the best in that person and push him or her to grow professionally?

"It is better to fail in originality than to succeed in imitation."

38.) Aside from your individual ability, how can you be of help in terms of team performance? What traits do you think you possess that could help your team to excel? What is the essence of teamwork for you?

39.) When do you usually help a colleague? Is there a limit when it comes to helping someone with his tasks? What could be the downside of always lending your colleagues a hand, if you can think of any?

"Success usually comes to those who are too busy to be looking for it."

40.) What traits do you believe a good leader should possess? Give at least 3 and try to elaborate each. Now observe yourself for a while, what particular leadership trait do you possess and how can you make use of it?

EMPLOYEES: *On Purpose and Self-Awareness*

"Success seems to be connected with action. Successful people keep moving. Of course, they make mistakes, but they don't quit."

41.) List down 3 passions, or any sort of interest you love doing the most. How do these activities make you happy? Despite your busy schedule and responsibilities, how do you try to squeeze in a quick "me-time" to unwind and do these activities?

42.) In what circumstance do you get most excited or motivated? How often do you feel this way? More particularly, when was the last time you felt excited about something, and what was it? How do you think exciting activities can be beneficial for you as an individual?

"One can have no smaller or greater mastery

than mastery of oneself."

43.) When was the last time you felt most engaged in your work? What were you doing then? What are the elements of a fulfilling job, in your own opinion?

44.) List down at least 5 people that you look up to as professional individuals. What do these people have that made them good role models? How do you try to be a good example to others, just like these people?

*"The people who succeed are irrationally
passionate about something."*

45.) In what way do you think your workmates would describe you? Are you worried that some of them may actually have something unpleasant to say about you? Or are you confident in your relationship with them? If so, why?

46.) Granted that you have enough time and money to do anything you want, what would you be doing at this moment? Who would you create experiences with?

"There is a powerful driving force inside every human being that, once unleashed, can make any vision, dream, or desire a reality."

47.) What was your first ideal job when you were younger? Did you really see yourself pursuing this career? How different is your first ideal job to the job that you have right now? What caused your change of mind?

48.) What is your own, personal definition of being successful? And at what age do you wish to become totally successful, both personally and professionally?

"Don't be afraid to give up the good to go for the great."

49.) If you were to leave your company tomorrow, what legacy would you leave behind? How would people remember you? What reputation have you built for yourself?

50.) On a scale of 1 to 5, how balanced do you think your work-life routine is? What do you think could be the reason for this? If your answer is 2 or below, how do you plan to change your routine in order to rebalance everything?

EMPLOYEES: On (Separating) Personal and Work-Related Issues

"Success is how high you bounce when you hit bottom."

51.) Do you have any worries at home or at work that you think should be given attention right now? How do you usually to fix issues without affecting the quality of your work or personal life? And aside from professionalism, why is it important to separate personal issues from work-related ones?

52.) Problems at home are inevitable, but how do you get to face your professional responsibilities despite carrying the emotional burden? When is the right time for someone to finally take a vacation leave and try to loosen up?

Try not to become a man of success. Rather become a man of value."

53.) Do you know anyone at work who may be emotionally burdened? If so, what can you do to try to ease this person's burden?

54.) What are the signs that a person is actually mixing up his personal issues with work-related ones? How can it affect this person and other people who are directly working with him?

"Success is walking from failure to failure with no loss of enthusiasm."

55.) What kind of support structure do you think emotionally burdened employees should have? How can a support group help in terms of lightening up this person's mindset towards everything?

"The master has failed more times than the beginner has even tried."

56.) If you were to teach someone how to lighten up, be happier, be more enthusiastic – or basically anything positive, what exactly would you tell this person? What kind of approach would you use in order to show how to be optimistic?

57.) If your superior were to assign you to organize a recreational team excursion, how exactly would you plan it? Give at least 5 fun activities you'd love to include and please elaborate on each.

"Celebrate your successes. Find some humor in your failures."

58.) If you were not in the current industry you're in, what kind of job do you think you'd be doing? How different would things have turned out if you landed on a totally different line of work?

59.) If you could go back in time, what particular regretful event would you try to change? What is your reason for choosing this, and how would it change the current situation you're in?

"Outstanding people have one thing in common: An absolute sense of mission."

60.) If you could be anyone influential for 24 hours, who would you choose to be? How would you make use of your time limit in making significant changes in people's lives (perhaps including yours)?

EMPLOYEES: On Financial Matters

"Many of life's failures are people who did not realize
how close they were to success when they gave up."

61.) At what age do you wish to be financially stable? What do you think are the common reasons that hold people back from becoming financially secure?

62.) What are the things you need to consider with respect to saving money? Do you have financial priorities? What are they? How can you improve them? How can you make better use of your money to achieve financial stability?

"Put your heart, mind, and soul into even your smallest acts. This is the secret of success."

63.) Do you think you are well-compensated for the amount of work and stress that you acquire on a daily basis? Salary is a common driving factor to keep an employee motivated, but when do you think salary alone isn't enough to continue working?

64.) What are the things that you prioritize when it comes to spending your hard-earned money? Are you usually willing to spend on your relaxation and leisure? If so, what could be the benefits of allotting a budget for self-pleasure?

"Success consists of going from failure to failure
without loss of enthusiasm."

65.) Is it really practical to accept a high-paying job with a really stressful nature? If you were given this offer, what factors would you consider before accepting or turning it down?

"The path to success is to take massive, determined action."

66.) How do you usually start your day, from the moment you leave your bed up until you reach the workplace? What activities take up most of your time every day?

67.) How do you budget your time in order to organize your daily tasks? What activities do you usually put on top of your priorities? Do you get to finish most of them, or do you often run out of time before getting things done?

"Successful people do what unsuccessful people are not willing to do. Don't wish it were easier; wish you were better."

68.) How can proper time management affect an employee's performance? What do you think are the usual factors that hinder an individual from managing his time well? Can you recall an incident wherein improper time-handling affects your performance so bad?

69.) What are the things you often prioritize during the work week and the things you prioritize during your days off? Do you think that taking home some work is reasonable?

"Only those who dare to fail greatly can ever achieve greatly."

70.) What is an ideal time management plan for you? Try to create a short one and explain in details. Then answer these two questions: In what way do you think this plan is ideal? What is stopping you from actually putting this ideal plan into action?

71.) Think of an activity that you have put off doing for a long time. It could be a particular task at work, a hobby, or just anything that you wish to do, but still haven't. What's stopping you from actually doing it?

"Always bear in mind that your own resolution to succeed
is more important than any other one thing."

72.) Do you write a to-do list? Do you think it is an effective way to keep track of your supposed activities for the day?

73.) Recall the last time you procrastinated. What was the reason for this delay and how did this affect you (personally or professionally)? Is it an isolated case, or are you really having a hard time following schedules? Please elaborate.

"Do you want to know who you are? Don' ask. Act! Action will delineate and define you."

74.) At the end of each day, are you usually satisfied with the number of things that you get done? How often do you feel productive? And what exactly do you feel about unfinished chores or tasks?

75.) Time management is a useful skill in any workplace, but how can it help you in terms of your personal life? Do you think time management is still necessary at home? How can you put this into practice?

EMPLOYEES: *On Getting Unstuck*

"Before anything else, preparation is the key to success."

76.) Describe your current work-life situation. How's that working for you so far? How exactly does the thought of getting up for work make you feel?

77.) On your days off, do you look forward or at least intend to do fun things to break your routine? Or were you simply hoping to catch up on your sleep? Is there anything in particular that makes you feel excited about going to work?

78.) Some people are afraid of changes; afraid of facing new challenges outside their comfort zone. How about you? Can you think of at least 3 things that you are actually afraid of? – Things that are probably getting in the way of your dreams, or living the life that you want?

79.) What elements in your life are you willing and ready to change? And what are those that you are not ready for at this point? What are the things that you usually consider before acknowledging that you are not ready for something yet?

"The ones who are crazy enough to think they can change the world,
are the ones that do."

80.) With all honesty, what bad habits do you need to stop doing? What makes it difficult to change or stop in the first place?

EMPLOYEES: On Constant Learning

"If you are working on something exciting that you really care about, you don't have to be pushed. The vision pulls you."

81.) Considering all the things you have gone through in the past 5 years, what life lessons have you learned? Among these lessons, what do you think was the biggest? How did it affect your life?

82.) What was the most significant wisdom you have acquired in your life? Did someone impose this on you, or did you acquire it from your own experience? Do you believe you're already wise enough to get you through hardships?

"Success is liking yourself, liking what you do,

and liking how you do it."

83.) How do you take criticism? What, for you, is the difference between constructive and offensive criticism, and how do you recognize them?

84.) When someone criticizes you, does it affect your confidence or lessen your motivation, in any way? Who do you normally talk to when you want to confide about not being confident on something?

85.) If you can share any of your experience and knowledge to the younger ones, what particular event in your life would you share? How would you relate this story to your audience in order to inspire them?

"Do not watch the clock; do what it does. Keep going."

86.) How different is your mindset this day from your mindset 5 years ago? What particularly has changed? And how did you cope with these changes? Do you believe you are in a better disposition this time?

87.) When you reach your senior stage in life, how would you like to look back? What exactly are the things you'd like to remember? And what sense of fulfillment do you wish to acquire by this age?

"When your desires are strong enough, you will appear to possess superhuman powers to achieve them."

88.) What life lesson do you wish you have known earlier? Granting that it's possible, what particular event in your life would you like to do over again? And what would you do differently?

89.) What kind of wisdom or lesson do you wish you could impart to people? In what way do you want to help those who are undecided about their career or personal life?

90.) Do you believe that there's always an opportunity to learn in every situation? How do you seek new knowledge or wisdom to further improve yourself?

EMPLOYEES: *Journal Prompts*

"The ladder of success is never crowded at the top."

In this part, we will complete the prompts provided below. It could be just a few sentences or an entire paragraph depending on how much you want to share. Nevertheless, I encourage you to go into details. Use no filter.

91.) I may not be perfect, but I always try to be the best version of myself by...

92.) I understand and comply with my obligations as a responsible adult, but I like to keep in touch with my inner child by ...

"All progress takes place outside the comfort zone."

93.) I am happy being around those I love, like...

94.) I believe it is important to take a break and make time for my passion which is...

"Don't let the fear of losing be greater than the excitement of winning."

95.) Failure is an important part of an individual's career and personal growth because...

96.) Finding and working towards our purpose in life is something we should never get tired of doing because…

"The only limit to our realization of tomorrow will be our doubts of today."

97.) We should have a good understanding of our financial health because…

98.) I respect people who...

"The way to get started is to quit talking and begin doing."

99.) Constantly growing and exceeding yourself despite problems and personal issues is important because...

100.) I can describe my life as...

LEADERS AND BUSINESS OWNERS: On People and Professional Relationships

"Success is a science; if you have the conditions, you get the result."

1.) How strict or easy-going are you with your employees? Do you try to interact with them when your schedule permits? Does being with your people contribute to your overall happiness in the workplace? Please explain.

2.) List down 5 employees or co-leaders whom you consider closest to you. How is your relationship with them? How can you improve it? How should an individual with a leadership role grow interpersonal relationships?

"The success of any great moral enterprise
does not depend upon numbers."

3.) What other interests do you share with your people that are not related to work? To put more simply, how do you get to know your people when you are outside your work/professional space? What would you recommend your people to do in order to unwind and loosen up?

4.) Give at least 3 kinds of traits that you look for in an ideal employee. How important are these traits to you? And how do you think these traits will affect the business in general?

"The ability to convert ideas to things
is the secret of outward success."

5.) Personal problems may affect an individual's performance at work. On a scale of 1 to 5, how open are you in terms of listening to your employee's personal issues? As their superior, what can you do to help them feel better about themselves?

6.) List down 3 major behaviors that you think people might not like about you. What factors do you think contribute to these behaviors? And as a leader yourself, how do you feel about these behavioral issues? Do you think it is something that you can actually work on?

"I measure success in terms of the contributions an individual
makes to her fellow human beings."

7.) What forms of body language do you consider as strong signs that people may not be happy about their job? If you see one of your workers showing these signs, what steps are you going to take?

8.) List down 3 misunderstanding incidents among your workers. As their superior, what did you do (or do you have to do) to help them resolve their issues? In events like this, do you think leaders should really step in? Please elaborate.

"There are no secrets to success. It is the result of preparation, hard work, and learning from failure."

9.) Think of any misunderstanding or argument you had with an employee. What was the reason for it? How did you manage to fix the issue without escalating the tension? Do you think you handled the situation fairly?

10.) Misunderstandings at the workplace are inevitable. As someone in a leadership role, what exactly is your mindset towards this? What can you advise your people in order to avoid miscommunication with their fellow workers?

LEADERS AND BUSINESS OWNERS: On Achievements and Failures

"Be a student as long as you still have something to learn,
and this will mean all your life."

11.) Reminisce at least 3 achievements you have acquired as a leader in the past couple of years. Which among these do you consider the biggest? Can you try to look back at some of the things you had to sacrifice or focus on in order to achieve them?

12.) How do you recognize an employee's small yet significant achievement? What do you do to help them come up with a fresher work perspective? How do you think small things actually contribute to a business' success?

*"I honestly think it is better to be a failure at something you love
than to be a success at something you hate."*

13.) How do you celebrate your team's achievement? How can you help the workers in maintaining their enthusiasm towards work? And what exactly is the role of enthusiasm in team productivity?

14.) How can you lift someone's spirit when he is being discouraged by his past failures? What piece of advice are you going to give this person in order to get him back on track?

"Never give up on what you really want to do. The person with big dreams is more powerful than one with all the facts."

15.) How did your past achievements change your perspective towards work? Was there ever a time that you felt like giving up? Did you ever look up at a certain leader before you became a leader yourself?

16.) How do you feel when a worker fails to deliver quality work? Do you normally get angry, or do you give this person a chance to explain his reason? How do you think leaders should handle disappointments caused by non-performing employees?

"Small daily improvements over time lead
to stunning results."

17.) Think about the biggest failure you had as a business person or a leader. What did you learn from this event, and how did this failure make you the person that you are today?

18.) How do you teach your people to take failures positively, considering that they look up to you during the tough times?

"Success seems to be connected with action. Successful people keep moving. They make mistakes, but they don't quit."

19.) Do you think that, as a leader, it is okay to share your own success story (success in terms of being promoted or chosen to be a leader) to those who are starting to lose hope? What is your take on this? Please elaborate.

20.) Some employees needed more time before he is able to adapt to his work environment. This sometimes leads to bad performance or quality of work. How do you think a one-on-one talk with this employee may help him do better next time?

"No one is unsmart. Everyone's a genius at something.
Our job is to find it. And then encourage it."

21.) What was your main reason for creating a team or business? Can you list down the primary factors that influenced your decision?

22.) Initially, when you first started your business, what product or service did you want to offer? Is the product or service you currently offer different from your original idea? How many times did you change your mind before you actually came up with the final one?

"Some people dream of success, while other people get up
every morning and make it happen."

23.) What is the added value that accompanies the sale of your products or services? What change or impact in the lives of others are you trying to pursue? Are you passionate about this cause?

24.) Were you ready to commit yourself – along with your time and attention – in order to be successful in the field that you have chosen? What were the first major setbacks and difficulties you encountered?

"The successful man will profit from his mistakes
and try again in a different way."

25.) How did your life change as a whole? Did you have to give up some of your hobbies or leisure activities? Did you discover a new sense of strength within you, or perhaps new weaknesses? Please elaborate.

26.) Handling a business could be very exhausting, and it is imperative that you be in a good mental, physical and emotional condition in order to run it well. How was your overall health status when you started working on your business? Has it improved? If not, what can you do to make sure you're operating at 100%?

"Twenty years from now you will be more disappointed by the things that you didn't do than by the ones you did do. So throw off the bowlines. Sail away from the safe harbor. Catch the trade winds in your sails. Explore. Dream. Discover."

27.) Getting your feet wet on a business venture requires being financially ready for the expenses that are about to come. How were you able to accomplish the financial requirements involving the business? Do you think seeking professional financial advice is really needed? What are your thoughts on this?

28.) Do you believe you possess all the necessary skills to control the operations on a daily basis? Or did you ask someone to help you out with it?

"As a general rule, the most successful man in life
is the man who has the best information."

29.) Do you consider yourself tech-savvy? Do you think you have an up-to-date knowledge of tools and applications that could make business run smoothly? If not, how do you plan to adapt to this?

30.) Do you think your academic background was enough to sustain your long-term business goals? Are you willing to get certifications or take short courses to widen your knowledge in your field of expertise? Why or why not?

"I learned to always take on things I'd never done before. Growth and comfort do not coexist."

31.) Despite many other similar businesses around the country, what do you think makes your business unique? What advantages do you have that may actually beat your competitors?

32.) Running a business will be impossible without your key players. How did you choose your management team? The operations employees? How crucial is it for startups to hire the right people, and most importantly, how can hiring the wrong ones affect your operations as a whole?

"I cannot give you the formula for success, but I can give you the formula for failure —
It is: Try to please everybody."

33.) What type of market do you target? And how, in the first place, are you planning to sell your products or services to this particular market?

34.) What are the elements of a successful business? How do we identify whether or not the business has the potential to be sustainable? And if worst comes to worst, when do we say that it is more practical to stop than acquire more financial damage?

"Success is not the key to happiness. Happiness is the key to success.

If you love what you are doing, you will be successful."

35.) How big, really, is the market you are trying to enter? How important is it to estimate the potential profit before actually getting yourself in?

LEADERS AND BUSINESS OWNERS: Running the Business

"Life shrinks or expands in proportion to one's courage."

36.) Write about your typical at work. Who help you run the business, and how are responsibilities usually shared?

37.) How do you address work-related issues? And as a leader, entrepreneur, or business owner, how crucial is it to fix misunderstandings immediately?

"You learn more from failure than from success.
Don't let it stop you. Failure builds character."

38.) Do you regret having or not having done something that relates to your business? Share how you would have done things differently if given the chance.

39.) Share with us one successful customer service story to inspire people to always give their best. Focus on the impact you have left into this customer's life.

"Integrity is more valuable than income. Honor is richer than fame.
Self-Worth is wealthier than net worth."

40.) Explain briefly how intricate it was to establish your own management team. Mention the factors that you had to consider.

41.) What are the things that have contributed to your success as a leader or entrepreneur? Did you ever encounter things that got in the way?

"Most of the successful people I've known are the ones
who do more listening than talking."

42.) How do you define being fair? How is fairness an essential part of anyone's success?

43.) How did your product or service evolve in the past few years? How did you and your partners – along with your workers – adjust to this evolution?

"Success comes from knowing that you did your best
to become the best that you are capable of becoming."

44.) Discuss one mistake that (almost) took its toll on the business, what particular decisions led to it?

45.) Behind every successful leader, owners or entrepreneur is a good mentor. Discuss the knowledge and wisdom you acquired from this person. How did you apply it to the business?

46.) What do you think is the biggest challenge in the industry you are in? How does it affect the employees, business owners, and entrepreneur in general? State your opinion.

47.) How do you think leaders and business owners should take advantage of technology in running a business?

"Success is not the key to happiness. Happiness is the key to success.
If you love what you are doing, you will be successful."

48.) Is it really helpful to follow prominent businessmen's profile (Twitter, Facebook, etc) online? How can these people influence our perspective towards the business? And if so, who do you think we should actually follow? Please elaborate.

49.) When creating marketing strategies, who do you consult first before coming up with a major decision? What makes brainstorming and extensive research significant steps in creating business tactics?

"There is no scientific answer for success. You can't define it.
You've simply got to live it and do it."

50.) Aside from the academic background, what personality traits do you strictly look for in an employee when you're hiring people? In what way are these traits important in the business?

51.) Tell us the story behind your brand creation. Reminisce the time when you were just considering putting together a team or business. What were the constraints you encountered? And what made you finally decide to go for it? How about the meaning of your brand name or logo?

"The key to success is to keep growing in all areas of life

– mental, emotional, spiritual, as well as physical."

52.) What are the elements of a successful product launching? List down at least 3 major steps that have to be taken into consideration.

53.) What traits should a strong-willed leader, business owner or entrepreneur have? How are these traits going to help you in the industry you're in?

"You've got to get up every morning with determination if you're going to go to bed with satisfaction."

54.) How is attending an industry-related seminar or conference going to be helpful for a business? Please look back at one particular event you attended in the past; what takeaways or realization did you bring with you upon leaving?

55.) What modern tools or form of social media can you use to let people constantly hear and read about your brand? What is your personal take on online brand advertising?

*"Success in any endeavor depends on the degree
to which it is an expression of your true self."*

56.) Share at least one thing about the industry you are in. It doesn't have to be a major company secret – just something that people outside the industry probably do not know about. What makes it interesting?

57.) When interviewing a potential employee: Give at least 3 major questions that you should ask your applicant – something not written in the resume. How important is it to actually ask these questions?

"I'd rather attempt to do something great and fail
than to attempt to do nothing and succeed."

58.) Reflection: Are you comfortable with the level at which business is operating at this moment? Do you wish to stay at this level, or do you plan on pursuing growth aggressively? How are your actions reflecting your goals?

59.) What made you decide to venture into the industry you are in? What makes it worth it, in comparison to others? And what makes it suitable for your personality and expertise?

"Success isn't just about what you accomplish in your life;
It's about what you inspire others to do."

60.) Are there any business sayings or quotes that you have tried to reflect on? How do they make you feel about your business venture?

61.) What do you think is the most challenging thing about your brand or industry? And how do you get to handle the stress that comes with it?

"Many of life's failures are people who did not realize how close they were to success when they gave up."

62.) How do you picture your brand in about 5 years? Try to imagine and put into words.

63.) If you can speak directly to your younger self, what particular wisdom are you going to share that would help him get through the trials and come up even stronger in the present time?

"Don't be distracted by criticism.

Remember--the only taste of success some people get is to take a bite out of you."

64.) Let's say you are not in your current industry, what are you doing instead? Was your current job even your first choice? Please elaborate.

65.) Should we ever be satisfied with the current status of our business or brand? What is the importance of constantly wanting to improve it?

"Good things happen to those who hustle."

I want you to answer this in a more detailed and personal way. This may work as a diary; no judgment, no particular answer – just you being honest with yourself.

66.) What is your WHY for your business? What made it worth the risk?

67.) Success, no matter how much we prepare for the trials, is never guaranteed. How do you prepare yourself for possible failures?

68.) Your life doesn't just revolve around the business; you have other responsibilities, too. How can you focus on one thing without compromising the other?

69.) A business startup is more like a trial-and-error. You're not sure about the outcome, but you're learning ways on how to strengthen your foundation. What is your image of a strong business foundation?

"Arriving at one goal is the starting point to another."

70.) Your target market or ideal customer has to have a clear understanding of the products or services you offer. How did you come up with your product's concept?

71.) You probably have other options, like working for a big company, becoming a freelancer, etc. But why did you choose to have a business in the first place?

"Success is achieved and maintained by those
who try and keep trying."

72.) An establishment's validity is important. How did you work on the legal requirements of your business?

73.) Having a business will make your schedule all the more hectic. Do you believe that having a business partner would make things easier, or you prefer being on your own?

"If we did all the things we are capable of,
we would literally astound ourselves."

74.) In order to start a business, one must have enough capital to take care of all the expenses that come with it. Should you, or other aspiring business people, consider applying for a loan to get started?

75.) It is not always going to be smooth-sailing. We know that problems are going to come up one way or another. Where or who can you turn to for help?

"You can teach a student a lesson for a day; but if you can teach him to learn by creating curiosity, he will continue the learning process as long as he lives."

76.) It is not every time that you are going to receive compliments from other business people. How do you take criticisms?

77.) Running a business requires speaking to a lot of people, and probably attending different events in hopes of expanding your network. How open and confident are you in terms of meeting new people?

"However difficult life may seem, there is always
something you can do and succeed."

78.) Any brand needs exposure and plugging. What is your approach to business advertising?

79.) How did you consider the location of your business? Is it something that you can set up at home for the meantime, or does renting a small business space sound more professional?

"There are no secrets to success.

It is the result of preparation, hard work, and learning from failure."

80.) Every business starts off small. But how big is an ideal startup for you, and how big do you wish it turns out in the future?

81.) We all want to have a sense of freedom in terms of handling our schedule and not having to follow anyone's instructions. What do you like most about being self-employed?

"A good plan violently executed now is better than
a perfect plan executed next week."

82.) Say, the business shows constant improvement, when do you think is the right time to expand your number of employees?

83.) You can't expect people to purchase your service or product if you cannot even talk about it in detail. How strong is your product knowledge and how can you differentiate it from others?

"Success seems to be connected with action. Successful people keep moving.
They make mistakes, but they don't quit"

84.) Your family is your most genuine support group. But is it okay to hire a family member?

85.) Proper behavior in the workplace contributes a lot to its success. How do you personally discipline (or what is your personal approach on) unethical behavior?

"Success is not built on success. It's built on failure. It's built on frustration.
Sometimes it's built on catastrophe."

86.) In a world where promotions and advertisements are better done online, how d personal recommendation and word-of-mouth work for you?

87.) With proper training and genuine care, there will always be good employees that will serve as assets to the business. How should we take care of talented employees?

"Perfection is not attainable, but if we chase perfection
we can catch excellence."

88.) Customer satisfaction, at times, can be elusive. How do you handle irate customers? How do you work on their complaints?

89.) Up to what extent are you willing to adjust in order to satisfy a regular customer?

"You have to believe that you are the one who creates your success;
that you are the one who creates your mediocrity,
and that you are the one creating your struggle around money and success."

90.) For startups, when is it safe to finally expand the business (Expand, like probably hire more people, open a second branch, etc)?

91.) As a self-employed individual, up to what extent are you will be hands-on just to deliver customer satisfaction?

"The most successful people are mavericks who aren't afraid to ask why, especially when everyone thinks it's obvious."

92.) What is your biggest fear about the business?

93.) Coming up with the business' overall concept requires extensive research. Do we really need to come up with a hundred percent original idea, or is it okay to get inspiration from other business establishments?

"Keep on going, and the chances are that you will stumble on something,
perhaps when you are least expecting it.
I never heard of anyone ever stumbling on something sitting down."

94.) What kind of lifestyle do you have at the moment? Does your business support or complement the lifestyle that you really want?

95.) Is your business something you'd still have the enthusiasm to run 10 to 15 years from now? Please do elaborate.

"I never did anything worth doing by accident, nor did any of my inventions come indirectly through accident, except the phonograph. No, when I have fully decided that a result is worth getting, I go about it, and make trial after trial, until it comes."

96.) Can your business operate without your direct supervision? Please set a sample scenario.

97.) What is one thing that you will NEVER give up for business?

"You know you are on the road to success if you would do your job,
and not be paid for it."

98.) At the end of the day, what three major things do you wish to learn from all the stress of running a business?

99.) Do you see yourself expanding the business through franchising and/or branches? Picture it out, then try to put your imagination into words.

"You know you are on the road to success if you would do your job,
and not be paid for it."

100.) Is it worth it for you?

Conclusion

I was recently in Quito, Ecuador in a massive convention for entrepreneurs. It had been 2 days already and I could feel my body using its last bits of energy. Suddenly I heard one of the speakers conclude his talk with the following:

"So, my friends, you have to learn to ask the right questions. Questions are very powerful tools for creating change. Ask yourself better questions and your life will improve. Ask others better questions and their life will improve. Always remember- questions are the vehicle of the mind. Thank you."

And so, came the inspiration to continue thinking up books that will help my readers question and assess different areas of their lives. Your career or business life is of extreme important as it affects directly other areas of your life. Unless we are conscious of the decisions we make day by day in respect of where we're taking our lives, we will continue living this area of our life in autopilot. Being conscious of our current state is the first step for change. Perhaps the second is asking ourselves better questions. I hope this book has helped you realize things about yourself in this area of your life. If you enjoyed it, we'd appreciate an honest review on Amazon.

Thank you,

Gerald

Made in the USA
Lexington, KY
02 June 2019